CHANGING
Families

Single-Parent Families

Barbara Sheen

ReferencePoint Press®

San Diego, CA

About the Author

Barbara Sheen is the author of ninety-nine books for young people. She lives in New Mexico with her family. In her spare time, she likes to swim, garden, walk, cook, and read.

© 2019 ReferencePoint Press, Inc.
Printed in the United States

For more information, contact:
ReferencePoint Press, Inc.
PO Box 27779
San Diego, CA 92198
www.ReferencePointPress.com

Picture Credits:

Cover: PeopleImages/iStockphoto.com

6: Maury Aaseng
8: RimDream/Shutterstock.com
12: iStock/Thinkstock Images
21: Steve Nagy/Design Pics/Newscom

27: Pressmaster/Shutterstock.com
30: Ingram Publishing/Thinkstock Images
41: A.Ricardo/Shutterstock.com
44: PictureGroup/Sipa USA/Newscom
47: Alpa Prod/Shutterstock.com
54: DigitalVision/Thinkstock Images

LIBRARY OF CONGRESS CATALOGING-IN-PUBLICATION DATA

Name: Sheen, Barbara, author.
Title: Single-Parent Families/by Barbara Sheen.
Description: San Diego, CA: ReferencePoint Press, [2018] | Series: Changing Families | Audience: Grade 9 to 12. | Includes bibliographical references and index.
Identifiers: LCCN 2017058282 (print) | LCCN 2017059061 (ebook) | ISBN 9781682823644 (eBook) | ISBN 9781682823637 (hardback)
Subjects: LCSH: Single-parent families—Juvenile literature. | Single parents—Juvenile literature. | Families—Juvenile literature.
Classification: LCC HQ759.915 (ebook) | LCC HQ759.915 .S156 2018 (print) | DDC 306.85/6—dc23
LC record available at https://lccn.loc.gov/2017058282

Contents

Chapter One

How American Families Are Changing

Layla was in middle school when her parents divorced. Before her parents separated, it seemed like they argued constantly, which upset Layla. After her father moved out, she worried about how her life would change. But things worked out OK. She now lives with her mother and her little sister, and spends every other weekend with her dad. Her mother takes good care of the girls. And Layla's aunt and grandparents help out, too. Layla admits that the arrangement is not perfect, but with all the arguments and tension, her life was not ideal before her parents split up. And whether her parents are together or apart, she knows that she is still part of a family that cares about her.

By definition, a family is a group of people related by blood, marriage, or legal bonds. Older family members typically introduce younger family members to cultural norms and moral values. Although there are many different types of families, when people think of a typical American family, they often think of a traditional nuclear family. That is a family consisting of a married man and woman, and the biological children they share, living together as a family unit. However, what constitutes a typical family has changed over time. As an article on the website of Family Story, an organization that supports diverse family arrangements, explains:

> Over the last 50 years there has been an explosion in the diversity of family structures in America. In today's America, there is no one family arrangement that the majority of children live in. Fewer people are getting married and more children are born to parents who aren't married. . . . These changes are part of the continuing evolution of America's families.[1]

Indeed, single-parent families, which are households headed by an adult that has all or most of the responsibilities for raising a child or children, are becoming more and more common. Approximately 27 percent, or 22 million, American youngsters under age twenty-one are currently being raised in a single-parent family.

Many Configurations

Single-parent families come in many configurations and form for a variety of reasons. Depending on the particular circumstances, they may be headed by a mother, a father, or another adult family member like a grandparent, and they may include any number of children. There are many reasons why a person becomes a single parent. Some individuals were formerly married or in a relationship that ended, leaving them with a child or children; or their partner died or had to live away from home for an extended period of time. Some single parents choose this lifestyle.

The most common type of single-parent family consists of a mother and her biological children. The US Census Bureau reports that 83.9 percent of single-parent families are headed by mothers. About 57 percent of these women are raising one child, while 43 percent are raising two or more children. The likelihood of being raised by a single mother varies by race. About 52 percent of black children live in households headed by a single mother, in contrast to 16 percent of white youngsters. Author Regina R. Robertson was one of these black children. She explains, "My mother raised me on her own, from day one. She's the only parent I've ever had."[2]

"In today's America, there is no one family arrangement that the majority of children live in. Fewer people are getting married and more children are born to parents who aren't married."[1]

—Family Story, an organization that supports diverse family arrangements

Percent of Children Living with Single Mothers and Single Fathers

The US Census Bureau reports that approximately 83.9 percent of children who live with one parent live with their mother. Approximately 16.1 percent live with their father. The bar graph illustrates the age distribution of children who live with one parent. It shows that a higher proportion of younger children, up to age eleven, live with a mother only, while a higher proportion of children between the ages of twelve and seventeen live with a father only.

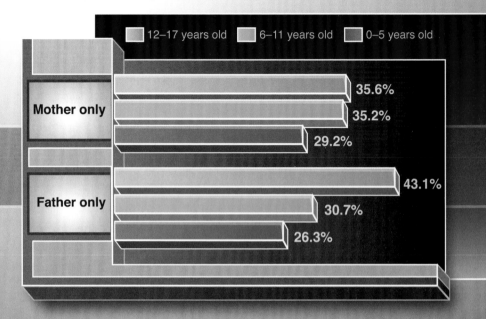

Note: Due to rounding, not all percentages add up to 100 percent.

Source: United States Census Bureau, November 16, 2017. www.census.gov.

Divorce

The majority of single-parent families form when couples divorce. The Center for Law and Social Policy reports that by age twenty-one, four in ten American young people will experience parental divorce. Currently, an estimated 44 percent of single mothers and 53 percent of single fathers are divorced or separated.

Getting a divorce is a legal procedure that ends a marriage. Couples divorce because of issues they have with each other, which can cause conflict in the family home and upset the children. As a nine-year-old boy explains, "Divorce is like two lions in a den attacking each other. You know somebody is going to get hurt real bad. All kids can do is sit behind a window and watch it happen."[3]

Many couples feel that they would be happier if they no longer lived together and that, in the long run, their children would be better off. "The atmosphere at home was very stifled and depressing with intermittent arguments and general unhappiness," a young man whose parents divorced recalls. "In the end I know [getting a divorce] was the right thing for them to do."[4]

When couples divorce, it affects their children in many ways. Divorce is a legal arrangement that sets forth rules concerning the couple's finances, possessions, and custody of the children. There are two types of custody: physical custody and legal custody. Youngsters live with the parent that has physical custody. This parent is responsible for the children's day-to-day care. The parent with legal custody is responsible for making legal decisions on the children's behalf. In most single-parent families, one parent, known as the custodial parent, has both forms of custody. Typically, the noncustodial parent has the legal right to scheduled visits with the children, as long as he or she pays child support. Child support is court-ordered payments made to the custodial parent to help support a minor child or children.

> "Divorce is like two lions in a den attacking each other. You know somebody is going to get hurt real bad. All kids can do is sit behind a window and watch it happen."[3]
>
> —A nine-year-old boy

A divorce decree sets down explicit conditions for visitation. The frequency of visits depends on a number of things, including where both parents live. Noncustodial parents who live near the children are usually allowed to see the children fairly often. One evening a week plus visits every other weekend are common. These visits may involve youngsters spending anywhere from a few hours with the noncustodial parent to overnight stays.

Although most youngsters enjoy these visits, for some kids, transitioning between homes can be challenging, especially if the visits involve spending the night. Young children often miss their home and custodial parent. A divorced father of two young children explains: "My son often says he doesn't want to be with me and would rather be with my [former] wife instead. At bedtime he often cries saying he wishes his mom was here to tuck him into bed."[5] Another challenge for kids of all ages is that the rules may be different in the two homes. Consequently, youngsters have to adjust to different expectations concerning their behavior, which can be confusing.

If the noncustodial parent does not live nearby, visits are usually limited to a few weeks during school breaks. This was the

Living with one parent but visiting the other can be difficult for children of divorce. Many kids think of their custodial parent's residence as home, so spending time at the other parent's residence can be difficult.

arrangement actor Michael Douglas grew up with. He recalls, "My own parents divorced when I was six. I was raised with my brother Joel by our mother on the East Coast, visiting my father in Los Angeles during holidays."[6]

Although many noncustodial parents are diligent about keeping in close contact with their children, it is not uncommon for the frequency of visits to decrease or even cease over time. Ongoing conflict between the parents, the introduction of a new spouse, job relocation, or personal issues can make it difficult for some individuals to maintain close contact with their child. That is what happened to actress Regina King, who says, "After my dad moved out . . . we'd stay with him every other weekend. . . . Then there was a shift . . . those every other weekend visits slowed down."[7]

Death

The death of a parent is another reason single-parent families form. About 1.2 percent of single-parent households develop due to death. Approximately 1.7 percent of these families are headed by widows, and approximately 4.2 percent are headed by widowers.

Having a parent die is very traumatic for young people. It can be particularly difficult for young children, who may not understand the concept of death, to accept that the parent is gone. As Lane, whose father died in a car accident when she was six years old, explains, "It was hard for me to believe my dad was really dead because I never saw him dead and wasn't even sure what that meant. So I held out hope for years that maybe it was not true."[8]

It is also difficult for the surviving parent to manage his or her grief while simultaneously adjusting to the new role of a single parent. In fear of breaking down in front of the children, some individuals

> "It was hard for me to believe my dad was really dead because I never saw him dead and wasn't even sure what that meant. So I held out hope for years that maybe it was not true."[8]
>
> —Lane, a woman whose father died when she was six years old

suppress unsettling emotions and encourage their children to do the same, which can cause youngsters to have emotional problems in the future. Rachel, a young woman who was fourteen when her mother died, explains: "The thing that makes you crazy isn't that your mother died, but that you can't talk about it and you can't let yourself think about it."[9]

Because it is often hard for the surviving parent to cope, teenage children frequently take on many of the dead parent's responsibilities in the household. This was the case for author Hope Edelman, who was seventeen and the oldest of three children when her mother died. She explains, "Almost immediately . . . I began driving my brother for haircuts, taking my sister to the dentist, and carrying the household's incidental cash in my wallet. I'd somehow stepped on a fast-forward button that transported me from seventeen to forty-two."[10]

Never Married

In some single-parent families, the parents have never been married. According to Child Trends, a research organization, 72 percent of births by black women, 66 percent by American Indian women, 53 percent by Hispanic women, 29 percent by white women, and 17 percent by Asian women occur out of wedlock. This translates to about four out of every ten births. Although not all of these individuals remain single parents, the US Census Bureau reports that about 37 percent of single mothers and about 25 percent of single fathers fall into this category.

Some unwed individuals become single parents by choice. These people are usually age thirty or older and are financially secure. To produce a baby, some women use a sperm donor, while some men hire a surrogate mother to carry an embryo that was inseminated using the man's sperm. Other individuals choose to adopt a child. "I want people to understand why so many of us are doing this," explains a single woman who chose to become a single mother through a medical procedure involving the use of donor sperm. "As I got older, and rarely dated, I got more and

Cultural Changes

In the past single-parent families were less prevalent than they are today. Cultural changes helped make single-parent families more common. Until the mid-twentieth century, for instance, sexual activity outside of marriage was socially unacceptable. Unwed pregnant women brought shame on themselves and their families. Typically, these women married the father, terminated the pregnancy, or gave the baby up for adoption. Keeping the baby and raising the child as a single parent was a rarity. Divorce, too, was not socially acceptable and was a last resort for unhappy couples. Indeed, many mismatched couples stayed together rather than face the stigma of divorce. On the other hand, modern societal attitudes toward divorce and sex outside of marriage have changed considerably. These lifestyles, which often lead to the formation of single-parent families, have become more socially acceptable.

In other instances, individuals are waiting longer to marry or are not marrying at all, but these people often want to have children. Consequently, many of these people are more likely than parents in the past to raise a child born as the result of an unplanned pregnancy or even to become a single parent by choice. Additionally, changing attitudes about gender roles has made it more acceptable for single men to raise children and for single women to take on the responsibilities of single parenthood.

more terrified that I would never get to be a mother. . . . I could not imagine being 45 and single and childless. . . . Today I'm the mom to a little girl . . . and I am happier than I could ever imagine."[11]

Most unwed individuals, however, become single parents due to an unintended pregnancy. Fifty-seven percent of out-of-wedlock pregnancies are unplanned, and many of these pregnancies occur in teenagers. The birthrate among teens in the United States is approximately 34 births per 1,000, or more than 700,000 births per year. Since an estimated 80 percent of teen fathers do not marry the mother of their child, many of these young women become single parents. As Vivian, a single teen mother, explains, "I thought and dreamed about marrying my baby's daddy and that we'd have a house with the white picket fence . . . and we'd live happily ever after. . . . None of that happened."[12]

In fact, it is not unusual for a child in this type of family to have little to no contact with the father. This was the case for rapper Eminem. "My father?" he says. "I never knew him. Never even seen a picture of him."[13] Moreover, according to the Centers for Disease Control and Prevention, one out of every four teen mothers becomes pregnant again within two years of the first birth. It is not uncommon for both teen and older single mothers to move from one relationship to another, producing children with multiple partners. These children are usually raised together in the same single-parent household.

Some young women become single parents due to unplanned pregnancies. Many of these pregnancies occur in teenagers, and the parents never marry.

The Challenges of Being a Single Parent

Being a single parent is not easy. Among other responsibilities, single parents are charged with raising children, managing the household, and handling finances with little to no assistance from the other parent. As Amelia, a single mother of two, explains, "There is no out. Being on 24/7 means that there is no one to pass the baton to when you are having a bad parenting moment (or day)."

With no one to share these responsibilities, single parents often feel overwhelmed. Many suffer from self-doubt. "It's so hard to know if you're doing a good job," says Sidney, another single mother. "When you're in a couple, you have someone who agrees (or disagrees) with your methods and can help you see the merit in your positive parenting moments and help you improve where you fall short. But as a single parent you have to do that alone, and it's not always easy."

Still other challenges involve financial concerns and making decisions alone. Yet despite these tests, most single parents do a good job. As Annie, a single mother of three, explains, "I try to remember that nothing is that big of a deal as long as I support and communicate with my children. Over time, I've learned to trust that things are all going to work."

Quoted in Nicole Caccavo Kear, "An Emotional Survival Guide for Single Moms," Seleni Institute. www.seleni.org.

How Single-Parent Families Live

As with all families, the way single-parent families live varies. Their lifestyle is largely dependent on the family's financial status. Some single-parent families are financially well off. Others struggle. Families headed by single mothers are most at risk of living in poverty. The US Census Bureau reports that 30.4 percent of these families live in poverty. One reason for this is that, according to the National Campaign to Prevent Teen and Unplanned Pregnancy, only 51 percent of teen mothers earn a high school diploma, which makes it difficult for members of this group to find a well-paying job. In the case of older women, many leave the workforce when they have children and depend on their spouse's income to support the family. If the spouse dies or the couple divorces, without recent work experience, these women are not always able to find a well-paying job. When single parents do get work, they may have to pay for child care, which can be very expensive. Moreover, some noncustodial parents (most of whom are fathers) default on child support payments or pay less than is required. Not surprisingly, many single mothers turn to public assistance to help support the family. According to the Census Bureau, 44.9 percent of families headed by single mothers received food stamps in 2016. Nor are families headed by single fathers immune to poverty. The Census Bureau reports that 18.8 percent of these families live in poverty.

To help support the family, many single parents work long hours or multiple jobs, which means they have less time to spend with their children. As basketball legend LeBron James, who was raised by a single mother, explains: "You would wake up [at] times and hope that the next day you'd be able to be alongside your mother because she was out trying to make sure that I was taken care of. But all I cared about was her being home."[14] Additionally, although many single parents make a big effort to attend their children's school and sporting activities, among other events, it is more challenging for them to do so than it is for two parents, who can share the load.

Even though custodial parents have to do the job of two parents, youngsters growing up in these families are usually well loved and cared for. As screenwriter and movie director Lisa Cholodenko explains, "No matter what kind of family you have—straight, gay, married, single parent, separated . . . if the bonds are strong enough, and the desire is there, you can get to the other side, still together and still a family."[15]

Chapter Two

How I See Myself and My Family

Growing up in a single-parent family has its ups and downs. Youngsters deal with many of the same challenges as kids who grow up in other types of families. For example, no matter what kind of household they grow up in, all young people face issues related to school, friends, and growing up. And sometimes they argue with their siblings or get annoyed with their parents. However, young people raised in single-parent households also face obstacles, cope with emotions, and may be involved in situations that are unique to single-parent families. All of this affects the way they see themselves and their family.

Fear, Guilt, and Blame

People who grow up in a single-parent family often have mixed feelings about their families and themselves. Fear of abandonment, for instance, plagues many youngsters. Kids who lose a parent to death often worry that something bad will happen to the other parent, too, leaving them all alone. Author and nurse Denna D. Babul, whose father was killed in an accident when she was a child, explains, "For a long time, I would freak out if my mother did not call me back immediately after I called her. . . . I have learned to talk myself out of the fear and to remind myself that it is over and most likely will never happen again. The little girl in me, however, is still scared."[16]

Death is not the only event that triggers this fear. Fear of abandonment troubles many young people whose noncustodial parent is out of the picture. These youngsters reason that if one of their parents deserted them, the other parent might do so too.

15

"Daddy left," says an eight-year-old girl. "Will Mommy leave me too? What will happen to me?"[17] These youngsters see their family as insecure and often cope with anxiety issues.

Feelings of guilt, too, frequently trouble these young people. Although children are not responsible for their parents divorcing, a parent dying, or a parent deserting the family, many youngsters feel that their actions or nonactions somehow caused the event to occur. They believe that if they had done something differently, their nuclear family would be intact. This feeling is so common that it is known as the if-only syndrome. As Sheila, who was fourteen years old when she discovered her mother dead from a heart attack, explains, "What haunted me for a long time was that I got there too late. My feeling that I could have saved her was focused on the moment that I found her lying in bed, and if I'd gotten there earlier she'd still be alive."[18]

Similarly, many young people blame themselves for their parents splitting up. They assume that some aspect of their behavior was instrumental in triggering the breakup. "If I had watched my baby brother when my mom was cooking dinner," one youngster says, "then, my mom wouldn't have left my dad. It's all my fault."[19]

Guilty feelings are sometimes mixed with a sense of relief. Although most children love both of their parents, if one parent is abusive or extremely sick, or if there is a lot of tension in the home, it can be a relief for the ordeal to end. Latricia, whose father was abusive and an alcoholic, explains, "My dad was an alcoholic and my parents divorced when I was eight-years-old. He died when I was eighteen from cirrhosis of the liver. . . . When he died it was kind of the closure I needed."[20] Although it is normal to feel relieved when a traumatic event ends, it can be confusing to feel this way. As a result, some youngsters see themselves as bad people for having this reaction.

Not Being Good Enough

Other emotions such as bitterness, anger, and low self-esteem sometimes arise when youngsters are repeatedly let down by an undependable noncustodial parent. Some, but certainly not all, noncustodial parents are unreliable. For a variety of reasons, these individuals continually break promises, fail to show up for scheduled visits, and miss important occasions in their child's life. Writer Sarah Tomlinson, whose father often did not show up for scheduled visits or call to cancel, recalls, "I spent more time waiting for my dad as a child than I ever actually spent with him."[21]

"I spent more time waiting for my dad as a child than I ever actually spent with him."[21]

—Sarah Tomlinson, author, raised by a single mother

Youngsters want to believe the parent's promises. On each occasion, they get their hopes up, only to be disappointed. Writer Danielle Rene, whose parents divorced when she was a child, recalls that her unreliable father repeatedly promised to send her gifts, visit, and call her, but he rarely kept his promises. "He disappointed me," she recalls. "That's what our relationship has always been, my father and me—an emotional rollercoaster of irregular guest appearances."[22]

Some youngsters make excuses for the errant parent, while others become distrustful or cynical. Often these feelings extend into other relationships, making it difficult for these individuals to accept that anyone, from a family member to a friend or lover, is fully committed to them. Says Rene, "My relationship with my father taught me that no matter how much unconditional love you give to someone, getting love in return was not a guarantee."[23]

Some develop anger issues toward the truant parent and cut their ties with that person. That is what thirteen-year-old Niko Amber did. She tried to be a good daughter to her unreliable dad but eventually became so frustrated with his lack of concern for her that she stopped seeing him. As she explains:

Good fathers are there for their children. They are supportive and engaged, and they know their kids' interests and do their best to accommodate them. Good fathers care about their kids' feelings, and most important, they don't walk in and out of their children's lives at will. That is the kind of father I deserve. . . . I don't have to be a "good" daughter to my father because he has never been a "good" father to me.[24]

Out of frustration, other young people direct their anger toward their custodial parent, who they blame for driving the other parent away. Usually, this anger is temporary. Others blame themselves. They react to their absentee parent's indifference by doubting their own self-worth. They speculate that there is some-

Lasting Effects

Research on the long-term effects of being raised in a single-parent family has shown mixed results. Some research suggests that children raised in single-parent households are more likely than other young people to do poorly in school, become sexually active at an early age, and develop substance abuse problems. Other research, however, finds little or no difference in long-term success rates between children raised by single parents and those raised in other types of households. The discrepancy may be due to a variety of variables. For example, some studies do not take into account the subjects' economic status. This is important because youngsters raised in poverty, no matter the family situation, face a greater risk of having difficulty in school, abusing drugs or alcohol, and having sex at an early age than other youngsters.

Another variable is the stability of the family. Children who grow up in a stable single-parent household in which they feel safe and secure appear to do just as well as youngsters from two-parent families. However, when young people grow up in an insecure environment, they are more likely to act out and have problems. Factors that contribute to an insecure environment include an irresponsible custodial parent who may have a substance abuse problem or a parent who tends to introduce a string of new partners into the home on an ongoing basis.

thing wrong with them that makes them unlovable. As Regina R. Robertson explains, "My father not being around wasn't something I ever really talked about. I thought it was embarrassing, and at one time in my life, his absence felt like a reflection of me. I remember wondering, 'How horrible a person must you be for your father not to care about you. '"[25]

Love and Pride

Even though some youngsters have a rocky relationship with their noncustodial parent, many develop a special bond with their custodial parent. After losing a parent, for whatever reason, youngsters often feel vulnerable. They depend on their custodial parent to fill the roles of both mother and father and to be there for them no matter what happens, even when that means the parent has to handle uncomfortable issues. In a letter to her father, writer Christie Lynn, whose mother died when she was a teenager, explains:

> It was hard when we were forced to discuss things that we both were totally uncomfortable with. But you have done great. Even with every mistake or every time you didn't think you handled something in the right way, you did okay. You have always been there for me. . . . You have shown me that with no matter what I face I won't have to do it alone . . . I am confident that it will be okay because we have each other.[26]

By taking on the job of both mother and father and supporting the family emotionally and financially, custodial parents help make children feel more secure. Indeed, many single parents dedicate their lives to raising their children and have little or no time for themselves. "You have to be everything," says Jessica McLaughlin, a single mother of twin girls. "Meanwhile you lie in bed at night, replaying the day in your head, questioning and second-guessing everything you do; sometimes with tears."[27]

As young people mature, many grow to appreciate the sacrifices their parent made for them. As a result, they view that parent with a great deal of admiration. For instance, when Kevin Durant was named the National Basketball Association's (NBA) 2014 Most Valuable Player, he gave an emotional speech thanking his single mother for all she had done. "We weren't supposed to be here," he said. "You made us believe, you kept us off the street. You put clothes on our backs, food on the table. When you didn't eat, you made sure we ate. You went to sleep hungry. You sacrificed for us. You're the real MVP."[28]

> "You have to be everything. Meanwhile you lie in bed at night, replaying the day in your head, questioning and second-guessing everything you do; sometimes with tears."[27]
>
> —Jessica McLaughlin, single mother of twin girls

Taking on all these responsibilities is no small task. Many single parents are stressed and overworked. Lacking a mate to talk to and share their problems with, some single parents turn to their child for companionship, sympathy, and support. They treat the youngster as an equal and discuss matters with them that adults do not ordinarily share with children. As a result, many single parents and their children develop a special relationship that combines a traditional parent-child bond with a peer-to-peer type friendship. According to writer Debolina Raja, "Children who grow up with single parents are often empathetic towards them. They understand that their single parents would need their companionship at home. This brings them close to their parents, paving [the] way for a strong bond of friendship. They depend on one another and are communicative and supportive."[29]

Although this closeness is usually a good thing, some single parents lean too heavily on their children. In fact, some youngsters come to feel responsible for their parent's well-being, which is an impossible mission. As they get older, some of these individuals hesitate to strike out on their own and do things like going away to college or getting their own apartment because they worry about leaving their parent without support.

Independence, Strength, and Resourcefulness

No matter how close single parents and kids are, they usually do not spend as much time together as do parents and kids in dual-parent families. In fact, children of single parents often spend lots of time without adult supervision. This is because most single parents work long hours or have multiple jobs, which keeps them out of the house. Many are unable to afford child care. Some youngsters stay with a grandparent or other relative or friend while the parent is at work. But many of these young people are latchkey children. These are elementary- and

Children from single-parent families often have more responsibilities than their peers who live in two-parent households. Some of these kids are expected to prepare meals, clean up around the house, and perhaps also help out younger siblings with schoolwork.

Gender Role Models

Parents are children's primary gender role models. Sons learn how to behave by copying their fathers, while daughters imitate their mothers. Youngsters who are raised in a single-parent household in which they have minimal contact with their noncustodial parent have only one primary gender role model—their custodial parent. This affects the way they see themselves and the way they interact with others.

Blogger Bob Alaburda, who was raised by a single mother, explains:

> When you have both parents, I imagine you get a more balanced view on dating and life in general. Growing up with a single mom, I disproportionately received the female perspective on a lot of issues. I feel like that's caused me to be more keenly aware of women's needs and emotions in relationships. Possibly to the detriment of knowing my own needs and emotions—it's impossible to know. I'd wager that someone growing up with only their dad might have a few more "manly" traits, while maybe not understanding or relating to women as easily. . . . Obviously, everyone is different, and the longer you live the more you can make up for these deficits. But don't be surprised if a dude with no dad never learned to be chivalrous, or a guy with no mom doesn't realize "I'm fine" means the polar opposite.

Bob Alaburda, "5 Things to Know About Kids Who Grew Up with Single Parents," *The Blog, Huffington Post,* August 11, 2015. www.huffingtonpost.com.

middle school–aged young people who regularly spend time at home, usually after school, without adult supervision while their parent is at work or otherwise occupied. This can be both lonely and challenging.

Without an adult to help them, latchkey kids have to learn to fend for themselves. For instance, writer and entrepreneur Jeff Charles grew up as an only child of a single mother. He spent a lot of time alone while his mother was at work. Although his only experience cooking was reheating food in the microwave, when he was eleven years old, he decided to make scrambled eggs. He called his mother at work and got directions. His first few attempts were failures. It took him a number of tries before he made an edible dish. But without an adult at home to cook for him, he eventually learned how to cook. Making scrambled eggs was just one of the many things he had to learn on his own. He explains:

> Growing up as an only child raised by a single mother wasn't easy. I had to figure out so many things on my own. I had to learn how to fight. I had to learn how to deal with people. I also had to learn how to be OK with being alone. I had to learn how to make scrambled eggs. Here's the thing. As much as she wanted to, my mom couldn't teach me everything the way she would have liked. And sometimes, she had to give instructions from afar. It was up to me to figure out how to put her instructions into action. I had to learn by failing. I had to learn by succeeding. . . . It taught me to be more independent.[30]

Indeed, because their parent is not home as much as two parents might be, these youngsters often have more household tasks than kids in other types of families. They may be responsible for caring for younger siblings, warming up meals, doing laundry, and taking care of their own possessions, among other chores. Contributing to the family in this manner provides most youngsters with a strong work ethic and a sense of pride. Many of these young people become more resourceful and independent than children raised in other types of families.

"Having no parent around a lot of the time when you're young means having to grow up a little quicker. It's not easy, but those tribulations give you strength."[31]

—Bob Alaburda, blogger and educator, raised by a single mother

And they often view themselves as strong and self-reliant. Says blogger and educator Bob Alaburda, who was raised by a single mother:

> Having no parent around a lot of the time when you're young means having to grow up a little quicker. It's not easy, but those tribulations give you strength. . . . We're more independent. . . . If you're the child of a single parent and you aren't in the upper class, you're probably a "latchkey kid." That is, you spend a lot of your after-school time unsupervised while your parent is working. You learn to cook, take care of your things, and otherwise fend for yourself. Years of that independence causes you to grow used to having alone time. I'll often feel guilty when my girlfriend helps me with something, because I'm so used to taking care of so many things myself. . . . I can't help it, and I imagine it stems from how guilty I'd feel if my mom came home from working her second job and I'd only created more work for her in the meantime while she was doing her best to provide for us.[31]

Growing up in a single-parent household has both benefits and disadvantages. Youngsters in these families deal with a variety of emotions and view themselves and their families in many different ways.

Chapter Three

How Others See Me and My Family

Single-parent families are viewed and treated by others in a variety of ways. Some friends, family members, and other caring individuals view and treat them with love and respect. These individuals understand the unique challenges single-parent families face and are a source of strength and support for them. But sometimes, these same loved ones openly disapprove of one of the parents, which can upset or confuse kids.

In contrast, some individuals, who may or may not know the family personally, accept as true unfavorable cultural biases and stereotypes that portray single-parent families as inferior to traditional families. And they treat these families accordingly. Author J.K. Rowling, who was a single mother at the time of this 2000 interview, explains:

> I think that my daughter is happy the way she's being brought up and I'm resistant to the way people say that is second rate. My personal view is that it's better for my daughter to be brought up in a single-parent family than in the context of an unhappy marriage. . . . Jessica [her daughter] has been a constant source of pride, joy and motivation since the day she was born, but I don't want her to grow up in a society that tells her that her upbringing is second rate.[32]

Still others view single-parent families no differently than they do any other type of family. In fact, in some communities, single-parent families are the norm. But whatever the case, how others see and treat them has a strong impact on young people and their parents.

Love and Support

Growing up in a single-parent family can be challenging. And being a single parent can be overwhelming. In many cases extended family members, friends, and neighbors, among other individuals, understand the challenges that these families face. They respect and care about the family and lend a hand however they can. From babysitting, to taking youngsters on special outings, and everything in between, these loved ones do whatever they can to provide the family with a supportive network. Although no one can take the place of an absent parent, these individuals help fill the void. As Mai Huggins, a woman whose father died when she was an infant, recalls:

> Because my father was gone, everybody stepped up. . . . Along with my grandfather—who, despite our generation gap was the closest I ever came to having a father figure— I grew up with four mothers: my mother, my grandmother, and my two aunts. I remember a time when I'd have to check in with each and every one of them, all the time, and about every single thing! But I knew that . . . they always wanted the best for me.[33]

In some instances a grandparent or another relative may live with the family, but even if they live at a distance, youngsters know that they can count on these relatives. Their presence in the family's life and their accepting and loving attitude toward the family help both single parents and youngsters feel more secure. As an eleven-year-old boy explains, "When everyone is fighting over who gets me and for how long, I call my aunt and ask her if I can come over and spend the night. We

Single parents often rely on family members or close friends to help look after their children. These loved ones help take care of the child and also spend quality time with them.

play games together. It helps me forget all the bad stuff that is happening."[34]

Ongoing Conflict

Sometimes, particularly in cases of divorce or abandonment, the very same people who support the family openly disapprove of the missing parent. They speak critically about the parent in front of the children, which can make youngsters feel uncomfortable or angry. Caught in the middle, youngsters do not know whether they should defend the absentee parent or remain silent. As Eva, a young woman who was raised by a single mother, explains: "My aunt has no qualms telling my mother that my dad is a 'no-good asshole' for my entire life. I know she does not like him, and I see why, but he is still my dad. Recently, I told her I was sick of it."[35]

Making matters worse, often one or both parents make derogatory comments about the other in the child's presence. Such comments, no matter who makes them, can make young people doubt their love for the maligned parent or lessen their admiration for the individual making the comments. Forest experienced this dynamic during his childhood. He lived with his father, and he frequently had to listen to his father's nasty comments about his mother. Influenced by his father's comments, Forest was hostile toward his mother. This made it difficult for

Grandparents Can Be a Positive Influence

Grandparents often play a significant role in the lives of their grandchildren and can have a very positive influence on youngsters who grow up in a single-parent family. Supportive grandparents provide their grandchildren with comfort, encouragement, and unconditional love, which gives youngsters a sense of security. In fact, research suggests that adolescents and teens ages eleven to sixteen in traditional, single-parent, and stepparent families whose grandparents are involved in their lives are better adjusted than youngsters whose grandparents are not. Young people with close ties to their grandparents are less likely to have behavioral or emotional problems than youngsters who do not spend time with or communicate often with their grandparents. They also appear to have better social skills. The benefit appears to be greatest for youngsters raised in single-parent households. A child's maternal grandparents—and the maternal grandmother, in particular—seem to have the greatest influence. "Grandparents are a positive force for all families but play a significant role in families undergoing difficulties," says Shalhevet Attar-Schwartz of Hebrew University of Jerusalem. "They can reduce the negative influence of parents separating and be a resource for children who are going through these family changes."

Quoted in Anne Buchanan, "Children in Single-Parent Households and Stepfamilies Benefit Most Socially from Time Spent with Grandparents," American Psychological Association, February 23, 2009. www.apa.org.

the two to bond. As a teenager, Forest began to question his father's negative attitude. He felt that his father's frequent criticisms of his mother had stood in the way of his developing a loving relationship with her. As a result, he lost respect for his father, and their relationship suffered.

Single Mothers Face Stigmas

Hostility can come from other quarters, too. For a number of reasons, some people view and treat single-parent families disapprovingly. According to sociologist, author, and single mother Patricia Leavy:

> Single parents get a bad rap. There's a cultural bias against single parents; an assumption that these households are . . . incomplete, and children suffer as a consequence. . . . I get very frustrated when people say things like, "but the ideal would be two parents." By that standard, single-parent families are always less-than. . . . I think the ideal is that children feel loved, supported and well cared for. That can come in, or be lacking in, any sort of family configuration.[36]

"Single parents get a bad rap. There's a cultural bias against single parents; an assumption that these households are . . . incomplete, and children suffer as a consequence."[36]

—Patricia Leavy, sociologist, author, and single mother

Families headed by single mothers, in particular, face stigmas. They are often viewed not as individuals but as a stereotype. That unflattering image is of someone who is lazy and unproductive and would rather take advantage of the social welfare system for financial support than work. While some single mothers do get help from social services, many work—and often at more than one job. Says Rowling:

Women like me . . . according to popular myth . . . [are] in it for all we could get: free money, state-funded accommodation, an easy life. Between 1993 and 1997, I did the job of two parents, qualified and then worked as a secondary school teacher, wrote one and a half novels and did the planning for a further five. . . . To be told, over and over again, that I was feckless, lazy . . . did not help.[37]

Families headed by single mothers sometimes face negative stigmas. People might believe that these children do not receive proper attention.

Other stereotypes depict single mothers as promiscuous and morally corrupt, especially if they had a child out of wedlock. As single mother Marissa Hicks explains:

> I adore my daughter and love being a mother. However, no matter how hard I work to improve my life I still have to deal with the social stigma associated with being a single mom. Personally, I married my first boyfriend with whom I first had sex with. People who assume that I am a single mom because I sleep around really frustrate and anger me. My friends joke around with me about the fact that they are proud I am in school and not stripping. Apparently, there is an assumption that typically single moms strip to support their children. Another stigma that gets under my skin is the comment I hear many men use, "single moms are easy, you know they put out." It seems to be a common thought that single moms sleep around looking for attention from males.[38]

Not only do these individuals view single mothers negatively, they also judge children raised in these families unfavorably. They assume that these youngsters do not receive sufficient care, attention, or discipline and therefore are somehow damaged. They believe that these children will struggle in school, have behavioral and emotional problems, abuse drugs, and become sexually active at a young age. Some children raised in single-parent households do struggle with these problems, but so do youngsters from other types of families. When people deem single mothers and their children as inferior to other mothers and kids, it can lower both the parent's and child's self-esteem.

"Women like me . . . according to popular myth . . . [are] in it for all we could get: free money, state-funded accommodation, an easy life."[37]

—J.K. Rowling, author and one-time single mother

It also increases the stress that single mothers face. According to Leavy, "Dealing with biases and stereotypes is depleting, and serves to tear single parents down, rather than build them up so they have the best chance of succeeding."[39]

Not as Competent

Generally, society views single fathers more sympathetically than single mothers. There are a number of reasons why this is so. One is that single fathers are more likely to be widowers than single mothers are to be widows, and the death of a spouse evokes sympathy. Another reason is that households headed by single fathers are less likely to live in poverty than those headed by single mothers. Therefore, they are less likely to depend on social welfare programs.

However, this does not mean that families headed by single fathers are viewed or treated the same as dual-parent families. Many people accept cultural biases that depict fathers as disciplinarians and breadwinners, not caregivers—a role in which single fathers are considered by some people to be inept. As journalist and single father William McCloskey explains, "Say 'single dad' and it's likely you'll conjure some lummox in an apron spooning scorched macaroni-and-cheese into a soup bowl for an ill-dressed tot with a bad haircut while the school bus beeps at the curb."[40]

> "Say 'single dad' and it's likely you'll conjure some lummox in an apron spooning scorched macaroni-and-cheese into a soup bowl for an ill-dressed tot with a bad haircut while the school bus beeps at the curb."[40]
>
> —William McCloskey, journalist and single father

These biases assume that single fathers lack parenting skills, are less nurturing than women, and are unable to deal with daily child-maintenance issues, such as cooking, shopping, caring for a sick child, helping with homework, and dealing with teachers and schools, among other things. Rich Holt, a single father

The Role Educators Play

The way teachers and other educators view single-parent families can have a positive or negative impact on youngsters raised in these households. Some educators accept negative stereotypes associated with these families. Among other negative viewpoints, these individuals believe that young people raised in single-parent households are not well taken care of, have discipline problems, have emotional issues, and are more likely to abuse drugs and alcohol than their peers. As a result, they tend to blame a student's educational problems on his or her family situation, whether or not this is the case. And they often have low expectations concerning the youngster's academic performance and general behavior. Being viewed in this manner can lessen a young person's self-esteem and negatively impact his or her academic performance. It can also stress single parents and make them feel disrespected.

On the other hand, many educators do not view young people raised in single-parent households negatively. Although they may be sympathetic to the challenges these youngsters face, they do not buy into negative stereotypes. They have the same expectations concerning these youngsters' behavior and academic performance as they have for young people raised in other types of families. Being viewed in this manner helps young people to succeed.

of two, complains, "Society expects women, not men, to care for children. And in the face of something different, people just ignore the facts and continue on with their ridiculous idea that the man in front of them is so incompetent and stupid that he couldn't possibly be responsible for anything good the kids have from braided hair to yellow belts in Kung Fu."[41]

In fact, the perception that men are less capable of being caregivers than women is so prevalent that it is common for others to expect the oldest female child in these families to take on her mother's role. It is assumed, even if she is a child, that she is better equipped to handle caregiving and household tasks than an adult male. For instance, when sixteen-year-old Mariana's mother died, her aunts and her father expected her to step in. "I was . . . cooking dinner every night, and trying to take care of my sister, who was always a wild kid," Mariana explains. "I was doing all the normal things a teenager is supposed to do during the day at school, and then I'd come home and cook and clean, like a mother."[42]

When people view single fathers as inept, it affects both the parent and the kids. For example, some individuals are reluctant to allow their children to have playdates in a household headed by a single father because they fear the children will not be properly supervised. Indeed, many single fathers feel like they have to repeatedly prove their competence to doubters, which is frustrating and stressful. Moreover, knowing that others consider their father to be inept can make kids feel embarrassed or ashamed.

Keeping Secrets

Nobody, including young people who are raised in single-parent families, likes being judged poorly. Most kids want to fit in with their peers. They do not want to seem unusual or abnormal. Nor do they want to be treated differently. Many youngsters worry that if other people knew more about their family, they might judge them or treat them unfairly. So, in order to protect themselves, they often keep information about their lives, which might embarrass them or cause them to stand out, under wraps. Some invent tales about their family in order to hide the truth. This is the case for Nisa Rashid, a teenager whose father was imprisoned when she was a little girl. She explains:

I always knew that he had been in prison, but I was never embarrassed about him being my father. What was embarrassing for me was knowing that my friends and

I didn't have the same type of home lives. A lot of them lived with their dads, and because I sometimes talked about mine, they'd ask me why he was never around when they came over. I didn't know how to answer their questions, so I'd always find a way to make light of the fact that he wasn't there at that moment. I knew I was the different one, which was hard for me to admit and accept when I was a little girl.[43]

Often youngsters are especially circumspect in cases in which they have been abandoned by a parent, an absentee parent is a substance abuser or a criminal, or the youngster has lost a parent due to suicide or violence. Some young people think that these situations reflect on them and are humiliated or embarrassed to speak about their circumstances. For many years this was the case for actress Charlize Theron, whose mother killed her father in self-defense when Theron was a child. "Everything changed for me that day my dad died. Years ago I used to cover it up and say he died in a car accident,"[44] she says.

Without a doubt, how other people view single-parent families has a big impact on the lives of youngsters growing up in these families and on single parents, too. Being judged as inferior just adds to the challenges these families face, while being supported and viewed with respect helps these families to thrive.

Chapter Four

Other People Who Have Had Families like Mine

On the surface, people like basketball legend LeBron James, actress/singer Selena Gomez, and swimmer Michael Phelps do not have a lot in common. Yet they share a bond. All three were raised by single parents. Like other individuals raised in single-parent households, they faced a number of challenges. But they managed to overcome these tests and become very successful. These celebrities and others like them attribute much of their success to the love and support that their custodial parent and other loved ones gave them.

Missing His Father

With a total of twenty-eight Olympic medals, twenty-three of which are gold, swimmer Michael Phelps is the most decorated Olympian of all time. But the road to success was not easy for Phelps. He was born on June 30, 1985, to Debbie and Fred Phelps. The youngest of three children, he had two older sisters, Hilary and Whitney. As the only males in the family, Michael and Fred were very close. They were best buddies who shared a love for fishing, sports, and video games. But this closeness did not last. When Michael was seven years old, Fred moved out of the family home, and Michael's parents divorced shortly thereafter. Too young to understand what divorce meant, Michael could not accept that his father was not coming back. He recalls, "I don't know if I had ever heard the words 'separation' or divorce before. . . . I heard my mom explain to me that my dad really wasn't going to live with us anymore, but it didn't make sense. Dad must have gone out to get something."[45]

Fred's absence hit Michael hard. The boy missed his father a lot. And as time went on, the older Phelps connected with his son less and less, which was difficult for Michael to deal with. "For me, not having a father always there was hard. . . . That was something that was a struggle for me,"[46] Michael explains.

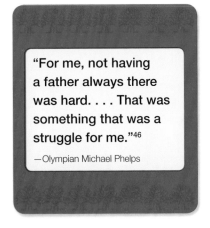

"For me, not having a father always there was hard. . . . That was something that was a struggle for me."[46]

—Olympian Michael Phelps

Making matters worse, Michael had problems in school. He was unable to sit still or focus his attention, and when things did not go his way, he had temper tantrums. His behavior was characteristic of an individual with attention-deficit/hyper-activity disorder, a condition he would be diagnosed with later. Once he began treatment, he gained more control of his actions. But until then, his odd behavior made him an easy target for bullying and teasing. As a result, he felt rejected by both his father and his peers.

Team Phelps

Michael's mother did everything possible to help him cope. His sisters were on a swim team. So, as a way to help Michael burn up excess energy, focus his attention, and take his mind off his father's absence, Debbie enrolled him in swimming, too. Michael fell in love with the sport. He was remarkably talented, and was soon competing against older children. But he did not forget about his father. Michael looked for his dad at every swim meet, but Fred was rarely there. Michael's two sisters and his mother, on the other hand, never missed a meet. They called themselves "Team Phelps" and did whatever it took to support the boy. For instance, Debbie, who was an educator, took on a variety of second jobs to help pay for Michael's training. She drove him back and forth to practice twice a day, every day, for years. And she worked closely with Michael to help him to learn to control his behavior. His sisters were there for Michael, too, cooking him breakfast and getting him on the school bus when Debbie was working.

When Michael was twelve, another person joined Team Phelps. He was swim coach Bob Bowman. Bowman became like a second father to Michael. "I relied on him for the kind of counsel a father gives a son. We talked about school, friends, family, girls, anything. . . . He has done more than mold me into a swimmer; he helped me grow up,"[47] Phelps explains.

Well-Known People Raised by Single Parents

Many well-known people grew up in single-parent households. For example, former presidents Bill Clinton and Barack Obama were both raised by single mothers. Clinton's mother was a widow, while Obama's parents divorced when he was two years old. Obama often talks about his mother with pride. "My mother was the one constant in my life," he explains. "When I think about my mom raising me alone when she was 20, and working and paying the bills, and, you know, trying to pursue your own dreams, I think that is a feat that is unmatched."

Other well-known individuals who grew up in single-parent families include hip-hop artists Mary J. Blige, Jay-Z, Sean Combs, and Kanye West. They are joined by other entertainers like Ariana Grande, Justin Bieber, Adele, and Alicia Keys, among others. Actors such as Julia Roberts, Keanu Reeves, Halle Berry, and Leonardo DiCaprio are also part of this group.

Many athletes, too, were raised in single-parent families. Eight-time Olympic medalist Apolo Ohno was raised by his father. Ohno, who has never met his mother, says this of his dad: "He's really been the backbone of my support group. He knows when I'm up and when I'm down." Other athletes who grew up in single-parent households include Shaquille O'Neal, Kevin Durant, Hope Solo, Alex Rodriguez, Colin Kaepernick, and Gabrielle Reece, among many others.

Quoted in Christina Coppa, "3 Successful Famous People Raised by Single Parents," *Babble*. www.babble.com.

Phelps made mistakes in his life. He got in trouble for smoking marijuana and for drunk driving. With the support of his "team," he took responsibility for his actions. Today he is married and has a son. His remarkable achievements as an athlete made him a national hero. But Phelps insists that he is not a hero. In his view the real heroes are his sisters, his coach, and most of all, his mother, who dedicated her life to supporting him. "Being a good athlete, a good actor, or a good musician who happens to be in the public eye doesn't make you a hero," he insists. "A hero should be somebody who can lift up other people with his courage and dedication . . . as I've been lucky enough to have with my mom."[48]

An Unstable Life

Like Phelps, basketball legend LeBron James was raised by a single mother. LeBron was born on December 30, 1984, in Akron, Ohio, to Gloria James, a sixteen-year-old unwed mother. LeBron's father was never in the picture. At first, LeBron and Gloria lived with LeBron's grandmother in the house where Gloria grew up. The older woman helped support the little family. She died when LeBron was three years old. Gloria tried hard to keep her family's home. But she could not make ends meet. She was a high school dropout who struggled to provide for them. She worked at multiple jobs, frequently leaving little LeBron unsupervised.

When LeBron was five, the city condemned and tore down the family home. With little money and nowhere to go, LeBron and his mother moved frequently. They often stayed on friends' couches and floors. He recalls, "We moved from apartment to apartment, sometimes living with friends. My mom would always say, 'Don't get comfortable, because we may not be here long.'"[49]

LeBron's life was very unstable, but through it all, he knew that he could count on his mother. "Whatever my mom could do or could not do, I also knew that nobody was more important in her life than I was," he says. "You have no idea how much that means when you grow up without so many of the basic things you should have. You have no idea of the security it gives you, how it makes you think, 'Man, I can get through this. I can survive.'"[50]

Gloria tried very hard to give LeBron a stable life. But things seemed to go from bad to worse. When he was in fourth grade, Gloria decided to find him a more secure home. LeBron was on a peewee football team at the time. The team's coach, Frankie Walker, and his family offered to take the boy in. According to Gloria, "It was the hardest decision I'd made in my life. But it was also one of the best. At that time in his life, he needed stability. It was hard, but I knew it was not about me. It was about him. I had to put him first."[51]

LeBron thrived in his new home. "My life changed," he says. "I had shelter and food."[52] He stayed with the Walker family through the sixth grade, seeing his mother on the weekends. He moved back with her once she found an affordable apartment.

Rising Up and Giving Back

While staying with the Walkers, LeBron joined a youth basketball team. It was coached by Dru Joyce II, who was also the head coach of the St. Vincent-St. Mary High School basketball team. When LeBron finished middle school, Joyce recruited him to attend the school and play on its basketball team. LeBron was a born athlete who averaged eighteen points per game. He helped lead the school to three division championships. When he graduated in 2003, he was the first player picked in the NBA draft. He signed with the Cleveland Cavaliers. He also signed a number of highly lucrative endorsement deals. Gloria and LeBron James would never have to struggle again.

Since then, LeBron James has won three NBA championships, four NBA Most Valuable Player Awards, and two Olympic gold medals, among many other accolades. He married his high school sweetheart, and they have two sons. He credits his success, both on and off the basketball court, to his mother's many sacrifices. To honor Gloria and help children facing challenges like those he confronted growing up, he established the LeBron James Family

Basketball star LeBron James grew up without a father. His mother struggled to provide for her son.

Foundation. It is dedicated to helping at-risk youngsters stay in school and be fit and healthy. As he explains, "I was one of those kids. Especially the underprivileged kids, the kids that walked the streets, that didn't have a lot growing up . . . so I can relate. . . . I'm here to help them."[53]

Best Friends Forever

Actress and singer Selena Gomez is another celebrity who was raised by a single parent. She was born on July 22, 1992, in Grand Prairie, Texas, to Mandy Cornett (now Teefey) and Ricardo

Single-Parent Families Throughout the World

Families headed by single parents can be found all over the world. Globally, children are more likely to grow up in a single-parent family in the Americas, Europe, Oceania, and sub-Saharan Africa than in other parts of the world. Children in the Middle East and Asia are more likely than children in other regions to live in a traditional two-parent family or live with both parents and extended family members.

Across developed countries, about 16 percent of all children live in single-parent families. The United States has the greatest percentage of single-parent families, with about 27 percent of all children living in single-parent households. At least 20 percent of families in Australia, Canada, Estonia, Ireland, New Zealand, South Africa, Sweden, and the United Kingdom are also headed by a single parent. These percentages correlate with an increase in divorce rates and nonmarital births and a decrease in marriage rates in the United States and Europe over the past fifty years. In many developing countries, desertion, death, and imprisonment are the main cause of single-parent families.

Globally, an estimated 85 percent of single-parent families are headed by single mothers. In the African nations of Ghana and Kenya, about one-quarter of all families are headed by women.

Gomez. Her parents were teenagers. They married after she was born but divorced when Selena was five. She did not fully understand what was happening at the time but knew she did not like it. "I wanted a family so bad. I wanted to have my mom and dad together. I remember just being angry with my mom,"[54] she says.

Although her parents were divorced, Selena was, indeed, still part of a family group. She was, and still is, close to her grandparents. And even though her father no longer lived with her, he remained a part of her life. But it was Mandy who was responsible for raising the girl, a task that was very challenging for the young woman. As Selena explains, "Having me at sixteen had to have been a big responsibility. My mom gave up everything for me."[55]

> "Having me at sixteen had to have been a big responsibility. My mom gave up everything for me."[55]
>
> —Singer and actress Selena Gomez

Mandy worked at multiple jobs to support the pair, but she did not earn a lot of money. Selena recalls, "I remember my mom would run out of gas all of the time and we'd sit there and have to go through the car and get quarters and help her get gas because she never liked to ask my grandparents for money. . . . I remember having a lot of macaroni and cheese but my mom never made it seem like it was a big deal. She was really strong around me."[56]

In her free time Mandy acted in community theater. She took Selena to her rehearsals and performances. The little girl loved everything about the theater, especially dressing up in costumes, putting on makeup, and playing a part. By the time she was seven years old, she was determined to follow in her mother's footsteps and become a performer, too. When the children's show Barney and Friends held auditions in Dallas, Texas, the little girl convinced her mother to take her to the audition venue so she could try out for a role on the show. An estimated fourteen hundred children attended the audition. Selena was one of the few chosen to be on the show.

Selena Gomez's parents were teenagers when she was born. Although the couple married, they divorced shortly thereafter. Selena was mostly raised by her mother and her grandparents, but her father continued to be in her life.

Selena appeared on the *Barney* show for two years but was eventually let go because the show was geared to very young children, and Selena was getting too old to be part of the show. In fact, although she loved being on the show, she was teased and bullied at school for being on a "baby" show. Mandy comforted her. She always knew how to make Selena feel better. Years later Selena would frequently say that her mother was her best friend. She explains, "My mom means my happiness, my love, my best friend and the world to me. She is the reason I smile and the reason I am here."[57]

Teen Superstar

Despite the teasing, Selena loved being on *Barney and Friends*. When her time on the show ended, she vowed to continue acting. Mandy supported her dream. She scrimped and saved so that Selena could work with an acting coach. Two years later, when the Disney Channel was holding tryouts in Austin, Texas, for new young actors, Selena and her mother were there. Selena did so well in her audition that she, with Mandy as her manager, was flown to Los Angeles for a screen test.

Selena did great. Disney signed her, and she and Mandy moved to Los Angeles. It was hard for Selena to leave Texas. She would miss her grandparents, father, and friends. But she had Mandy to guide her and keep her from being lonely.

Selena had a number of small roles in a variety of Disney television shows. When she was twelve years old, Disney cast her in a new show called *Wizards of Waverly Place*. The show was a huge hit. In the next few years, Selena's popularity and fame skyrocketed. Gomez appeared on television and in movies, formed a band that produced hit tunes, started a production company and a fashion line, and won multiple awards.

As a teen superstar, it would have been easy for Selena to become spoiled and self-absorbed. But her mother kept her grounded. Selena recalls, "Before we got to California, she told me, 'You're going to hear the word yes a lot. You're this. You're that. Yes-yes-yes. So I'm the one who's going to tell you no—only because I love who you are now, and I don't want you to change.'"[58]

By all accounts, Gomez has remained the same sweet-natured, down-to-earth person she has always been. Although she replaced her mother as her manager with a professional team, this did not affect their relationship. In 2017 when Selena, who was diagnosed with lupus, underwent a successful kidney transplant, Mandy was right by her side. The two have been through a lot together. They are still, and, probably always will be, best friends.

Indeed, like many youngsters raised in single-parent households, Selena Gomez, LeBron James, and Michael Phelps faced many challenges. With the loving support of their single parents, they, like many other young people growing up in these families, have managed to turn their dreams into reality.

Chapter Five

What It Is like When My Family Grows

Like most people, single parents enjoy the companionship of other people their age. They often date, form relationships, and cohabit with or marry someone other than their child's other biological parent. Single parents, according to writer Sabrina Toucinho, "have adult needs for intimacy, understanding, companionship, reassurance, encouragement and romance that can only be fulfilled by another adult."[59] However, when single parents introduce new people into the family mix, it changes family dynamics and raises many issues for young people.

When Single Parents Date

When a single parent dates, kids are affected in a variety of ways. Some youngsters are jealous of the new person in their parent's life. They see that person as competition for their parent's love and attention. For example, Steve, a divorced, noncustodial parent, included his dating partner, Casandra, in the activities he had planned during his children's scheduled visits. Since they did not see their dad often, the children resented sharing their father with her. As fourteen-year-old Tim explains, "We get to see him two days a month. Couldn't he be with just us? He has all the rest of the month to be with Casandra. We don't even get to talk to him."[60]

Having a parent date also causes some young people to worry about being abandoned. Thirteen-year-old Michael was one of these youngsters. After his mother left the family, he lived with his father. The two did everything together. They especially enjoyed going to movies and car races. When his father started dating Martha, things changed. Martha had no children and did not enjoy spending time with Michael. But she did like going to car races and movies. So, instead of doing these activities with Michael, his dad did them with Martha, and Michael was left to fend for himself. Because Martha did not appear to like Michael, he worried that if she and his dad became serious and decided to move in together, he would be sent to live with his grandparents. The couple broke up before Michael's fears could be realized. But the boy coped with a lot of anxiety while the couple was dating.

In addition to these feelings, many children of divorce retain the hope that their parents will eventually reconcile. Once either parent begins dating, the possibility of this happening lessens,

Some divorced parents eventually seek romantic relationships for comfort and companionship. Dating can be difficult for children of divorce to accept.

disappointing hopeful kids. That is how Kaylah, an Australian teen, feels:

> My mum and Dad broke up 1 year ago. . . . I just recently found my mum on a dating website talking to guys. . . . I see some of my friends with parents that are divorced then remarried with another man/woman & they are happy but I just cannot [bear] the thought of my mum or dad with anyone but each other. I get really anxious and scared that mum will get with someone else. . . . I want her to be happy, but I want her to be happy with my dad, not anyone else!!"[61]

Moreover, when a parent dates, some young people feel disloyal to their other parent if they like their parent's dating partner. According to author and family therapist Ron L. Deal, "Liking a parent's dating partner sometimes creates a loyalty problem for kids: They don't know how to embrace everyone and not hurt feelings (especially the other biological parent). Because they are caught in a loyalty conflict, children sometimes warm up nicely to the person you are dating and then turn cold. . . . Confusion comes with the territory."[62]

It is not uncommon for kids to try to sabotage their parent's new relationship by acting obnoxious, rude, or openly hostile toward their parent's dating partner. Corinne, a young woman raised by her father, recalls:

> "Liking a parent's dating partner sometimes creates a loyalty problem for kids: They don't know how to embrace everyone and not hurt feelings (especially the other biological parent)."[62]
>
> —Ron L. Deal, author and marriage and family therapist

> My father had sat my older brother and I down one night and asked us permission to date and I thought, "He's got to be kidding. Date? My father?" I guess because I didn't say anything, he figured I was fine with it. The minute that

woman walked through the door, I didn't want a thing to do with her. He was furious with me, and we fought about it all the time. He only dated her for six months, until she broke it off. I was so cruel to her. I think I might have been part of the reason why she left him.[63]

Children Want Their Parents to Be Happy

Not all young people have negative feelings about their parent dating. Children want their parents to be happy. Many are glad when their parent finds a companion who makes them happy, especially

Innovative Living Arrangements

Some single mothers have added new people to their families in an innovative way. They share a house and daily life with another single mother and her children. The mothers team up, sharing household responsibilities, child care duties, and living expenses, and they pool their finances. Sharing responsibilities like cooking, cleaning, shopping, carpooling, and doing laundry helps lighten their daily burden. Sharing the cost of rent and daily expenses allows the women to afford a better home in a safer neighborhood and better school district. Moreover, living with another adult helps relieve feelings of isolation and loneliness that many single mothers face.

Before becoming housemates, the mothers are often strangers. One way they find each other is through an online organization named CoAbode that acts as a matchmaker. It works much like a dating app. Interested single mothers register with the website and fill out a personal profile questionnaire. Profiles, which can be changed or updated at any time, are shared with other applicants so that applicants can identify potentially compatible matches who share their interests, values, and parenting philosophy. Potential housemates get to know each other via texts, e-mails, and phone calls, and by meeting in person. The children are introduced to each other through joint family outings. If everyone hits it off, the two families may choose to become housemates.

if the parent has had a difficult time being without a mate. Sixteen-year-old Lauren felt this way when her widowed mother began to date. She insists: "Your parent just has to have some fun time to get things off their minds.!!"[64]

Additionally, in cases in which parents rely heavily on their children for emotional support and companionship, some youngsters are pleased that their parent now has someone else to occupy their time. In fact, some young people are so eager to have their parent date that they try to act as matchmakers, especially if they would like to have another adult male or female figure in their lives. They may try to pair their parent with a single adult they admire, such as a favorite teacher, coach, or a friend's single parent.

Overnight Guests

It is not uncommon for dating couples to have a sexual relationship, which raises other issues. For example, if the parent has encouraged the kids to remain celibate until they marry, some young people can be confused and upset by the seeming moral reversal in the parent's behavior. As a result, these youngsters feel like their parent is a hypocrite. They feel like they can no longer trust the parent, and they wonder if they ever could. "Was the old Mom just hiding under the real one that is coming out now?" a young man asks. "Was I just not seeing what I didn't want to see? And, if that's true, then how am I supposed to trust what I think I see now?"[65]

> "My mother dated. A lot. There were always men in and out of our house, and I never felt safe."[66]
>
> —Nicole Shealey, a woman raised by a single mother

Other concerns arise when youngsters find their parent's overnight guest in the family home in the morning. Teenage girls, in particular, often feel uneasy about being around a strange man, who may view them more like a woman than a minor. This was the situation Nicole Shealey, a young woman who was raised by a single mother, faced. She explains, "My mother dated. A lot. There were always men in and out of our house, and I never felt safe."[66]

In other instances some youngsters develop an emotional attachment to their parent's lover. Although most dating relationships are temporary, these kids think of this individual as a permanent part of the family. If the couple breaks up, the child may feel abandoned and must deal with losing yet another beloved person. Since it is common for single parents to have several dating relationships in their lives, some youngsters are repeatedly hurt in this manner.

Stepparents

Dating often leads to marriage. According to the US Census Bureau, over 50 percent of US families are remarried or recoupled. About half of all youngsters growing up in a single-parent family are likely to have at least one stepparent at some point in their lives. Moreover, since an estimated 66 percent of new marriages involving children break up and many individuals remarry more than once, some young people have multiple stepparents while growing up.

When a parent remarries, young people often have mixed feelings. Although they know they should be happy for their parent, many kids cannot help but be upset, worried, or sad at the prospect. Many youngsters are content with the status quo and do not want it to change. On a practical level, they worry that the new family may have to move, which will disrupt their lives. For children of divorce or abandonment, having a parent remarry shatters any fantasies they may have about their biological parents reuniting. "It was just as sad as Grandma's funeral," ten-year-old Jacob says of his father's remarriage. "I knew it meant we could never all be together again as a family."[67]

Knowing that the marriage upsets their other biological parent presents another problem for many youngsters. These kids feel conflicted if they are happy for the newlyweds. One thirteen-year-old girl recalls, "I cried for two hours before the ceremony the day my dad and stepmom got married. I told them it was because I just

Preferential Treatment

When two single parents marry, their children become stepsiblings. Like biological siblings, stepsiblings often vie for parental attention. Although not all stepparents show overt favoritism toward their biological children, some parents may, knowingly or unconsciously, give their biological children preferential treatment over their stepchildren.

In the book *The Fatherless Daughter Project*, a young woman named Anna whose parents divorced when she was four and whose mother remarried a few years later explains her experience with a new stepfather and stepbrother. Anna recalls:

> My parents divorced when I was four, and Mom got custody of me and my sister. Dad moved to another state. . . . We visited dad twice a year, with little communication in between. Mom finally remarried just after I turned six, and we got a little brother in the deal. Our stepdad . . . made it pretty clear that he preferred his son [Jack] over us—it was just how it was. We knew we were not really his daughters, and although I deeply wanted to be Daddy's little girl, it never happened. There was always this distance between us. It was just understood that he was Jack's real dad and we were not blood family. Mom kept trying to make it look pretty from the outside, but on the inside we felt rejected.

Quoted in Denna D. Babul and Karin Luise, *The Fatherless Daughter Project*. New York: Penguin Random House, 2016, pp. 115–16.

got my ears pierced and they still hurt, but I was crying because I knew my mother was home crying."[68]

In families in which one parent died, youngsters whose remaining parent remarries often feel that their parent is attempting to replace the deceased parent and erase all traces of that person. In an effort to keep their dead parent's memory alive, these young people are frequently hostile or rejecting toward the marriage, their biological parent, and the parent's new spouse. For example, Audrey's mother died when she was fourteen years old. Six months later, her father remarried. She recalls:

> I went through an enormous rebellion against him at fifteen. It was like, Father with another woman? And she had two kids. I thought, "Who is this person in my father's life with all her tagalongs, and what makes her think she can become part of my life, too?" I gave her a really hard time until after I left for college. Now I think of her as my father's wife, and as long as she doesn't try to be my mother, we can get along fine.[69]

Adjusting to a Stepparent

It usually takes kids about two years to adjust to a stepparent. And some never do. According to the American Psychological Association, young children and older teens adjust more easily than youngsters ages ten to fourteen. This may be because young children are usually accepting of new people in the family, and older teens are fairly independent and are therefore less involved with the stepparent. Generally, kids adjust more easily if the stepparent does not try to assume a parental role but rather leaves parental decisions to the biological parent. This is especially true when it comes to dealing with issues related to setting rules and meting out discipline. It is not uncommon for kids to question a stepparent's authority, informing the stepparent that he or she is not their *real* parent. As nine-year-old Cindy explains:

> Every Friday on the way to pick up me and my brother, my dad would pick up a pizza for dinner. We would go back to his place, eat pizza, watch a movie and camp out in the living room. Now Judy [Cindy's stepmother] says pizza isn't healthy every weekend and that dad and her have to sleep in their bedroom. In my mind, she is changing the best parts of seeing my dad and he just goes along with it. I feel like he is letting her make all the rules. I hate it.[70]

Over time, many stepparents gain the trust of their stepchildren and develop strong bonds with the children.

After a period of adjustment, many young people come to accept, trust, and love their stepparent. Although they can never replace a biological parent, many stepparents help fill the gap. Indeed, some young people see their stepparent as a role model of what a good parent should be. As actress and writer Cindy M. Birch explains:

After my parents divorced, my mother remarried when I was eleven. She'd met a man who always treated her like a queen. This gentle giant stepped right in to fill the void of my absent father, too. Not only was he deliberate about making a positive impact on my self-esteem and shaping my outlook on male-female relationships, he also demonstrated, daily, what a man should be and do for his family. He was the one who walked me down the aisle on my wedding day, too.[71]

Stepsiblings and Half Siblings

Many stepparents have children from a former relationship that become part of the new family. And new half siblings are often added. So, besides adjusting to stepparents, many youngsters gain stepsiblings, as well as half siblings, when their parents remarry. Whether or not these siblings live with the new family or visit frequently, they change family dynamics and become part of a young person's life. For instance, the addition of more people in the family can make homes crowded. Youngsters may be forced to share their room, toys, clothes, and more importantly, their parent's attention with their new siblings. This can make young people angry and resentful. Resentment and jealousy also arise when stepsiblings and half siblings live with a youngster's noncustodial parent and get to spend more time with that parent than the parent's biological children do. After her father remarried, this was the situation that Alysse ElHage, editor of the Institute for Family Studies blog, faced. She explains, "Once my [half] brother and sisters were born, everything really shifted. My father tried to make me feel like part of his new family, but I increasingly felt like an outsider as I watched him be the full-time father to my siblings, it was really hard for me to share what little time I had with my father with anyone else—including them."[72]

Despite negative feelings, lots of stepsiblings and half siblings form strong bonds. Some older siblings become quite protective of their younger stepsiblings and half siblings. For example, as a boy, after his widowed mother remarried, former president Bill Clinton was repeatedly abused by his stepfather. Clinton did not try to defend himself. But when the man started to abuse Clinton's half brother, Clinton defended the younger boy. Indeed, many youngsters do not distinguish between their siblings, whether natural, half, or step. They are all part of the same family. The experiences that they share connect them forever. As Sharmayne, a woman who is raising her biological son and stepson together, says, "It takes more than blood to be a family."[73]

Source Notes

Chapter One: How American Families Are Changing

1. Family Story, "Why Family Story?," 2017. www.familystory project.org.
2. Regina R. Robertson, ed., *He Never Came Home*. Chicago: Bolden, 2017, p. 1.
3. Quoted in Laurene Johnson and Georglyn Rosenfeld, *Divorced Kids*. New York: Fawcett Crest, 1990, p. 7.
4. Quoted in *Huffington Post*, "5 Reasons Kids from Unhappy Homes Say It's Better to Divorce than Stay Married," January 27, 2014. www.huffingtonpost.com.
5. Quoted in Jackie Pilossoph, "Newly Separated Man Seeks Custody Advice," *Divorce Guy Grinning* (blog), October 4, 2014. www.divorcedguygrinning.com.
6. Quoted in Brainy Quotes, "I Was Raised." www.brainyquote .com.
7. Quoted in Robertson, *He Never Came Home*, pp. 83–84.
8. Quoted in Denna D. Babul and Karin Luise, *The Fatherless Daughter Project*. New York: Penguin Random House, 2016, p. 39.
9. Quoted in Hope Edelman, *Motherless Daughters*. Reading, MA: Addison-Wesley, 1994, p. 11.
10. Edelman, *Motherless Daughters*, p. 52.
11. Quoted in Single Mothers by Choice, "From a Mom of a Little One Through Anonymous Donor IVF," October 6, 2017. www.singlemothersbychoice.org.
12. Quoted in Candie's Foundation, "Diary of a Teen Mom, Interview with Vivian De Leon," 2015. www.candiesfoundation .org.
13. Quoted in Search Quotes, "Never Met My Father Quotes," 2017. www.searchquotes.com.
14. Quoted in Brainy Quotes, "Single Parent Quotes." www .brainyquote.com.
15. Quoted in Brainy Quotes, "Single Parent Quotes."

Chapter Two: How I See Myself and My Family

16. Babul and Luise, *The Fatherless Daughter Project*, p. 43.
17. Quoted in Johnson and Rosenfeld, *Divorced Kids*, p. 5.
18. Quoted in Edelman, *Motherless Daughters*, p. 81.
19. Quoted in Johnson and Rosenfeld, *Divorced Kids*, p. 29.
20. Quoted in Babul and Luise, *The Fatherless Daughter Project*, p. 66.
21. Quoted in Robertson, *He Never Came Home*, p. 62.
22. Quoted in Robertson, *He Never Came Home*, p. 24.
23. Quoted in Robertson, *He Never Came Home*, p. 26.
24. Quoted in Robertson, *He Never Came Home*, p. 13.
25. Robertson, *He Never Came Home*, p. 3.
26. Christie Lynn, "To My Dad Who Had to Finish Raising Me Without My Mom," Pucker Mob. www.puckermob.com.
27. Quoted in Pamme Boutselis, "Three Families, Three Stories: Raising Kids as a Single Parent," Parenting New Hampshire, November 2014. www.parentingnh.com.
28. Quoted in Ivan Angelo de Lara, "Single Moms Behind World-Famous Athletes," *Inquirer.net*, May 1, 2014. http://sports.inquirer.net.
29. Debolina Raja, "5 Advantages & 5 Disadvantages of Single Parenting," Mom Junction, January 27, 2017. www.momjunction.com.
30. Jeff Charles, "A Story About Scrambled Eggs and a Message to Single Mothers," *Huffington Post*, April 12, 2016. www.huffingtonpost.com.
31. Bob Alaburda, "5 Things to Know About Kids Who Grew Up with Single Parents," *The Blog*, *Huffington Post*, August 11, 2015. www.huffingtonpost.com.

Chapter Three: How Others See Me And My Family

32. Quoted in Jojo Moyes, "The Myths of Single Mothers, as Told by JK Rowling," *Independent* (London), October 4, 2000. www.independent.co.uk.
33. Quoted in Robertson, *He Never Came Home*, p. 171.
34. Quoted in Johnson and Rosenfeld, *Divorced Kids*, p. 172.
35. Quoted in Babul and Luise, *The Fatherless Daughter Project*, p. 119.

36. Patricia Leavy and Donna Y. Ford, "A Conversation About Single Parenting: Challenging the Stereotypes," *Huffington Post*, January 15, 2016. www.huffingtonpost.com.
37. Quoted in Katie Roiphe, "Two Kids, Two Fathers, No Problem," *Guardian* (Manchester), June 22, 2013. www.theguardian.com.
38. Marissa Hicks, "The Single Mother Battle on Stereotypes," Battered Women's Support Services, September 14, 2012. www.bwss.org.
39. Leavy and Ford, "A Conversation About Single Parenting."
40. William McCloskey, "Adventures in Single Parenting," *Parenting* (blog), *New York Times*, May 21, 2010. https://parenting.blogs.nytimes.com.
41. Quoted in Molly Smith, "Single Dads Speak Out," All Parenting, July 3, 2013. http://allparenting.com.
42. Quoted in Edelman, *Motherless Daughters*, p. 53.
43. Quoted in Robertson, *He Never Came Home*, pp. 69–70.
44. Quoted in Babul and Luise, *The Fatherless Daughter Project*, p. xxii.

Chapter Four: Other People Who Have Families like Mine

45. Michael Phelps and Brian Cazeneuve, *Beneath the Surface*. Champaign, IL: Sports, 2008, p. 14.
46. Quoted in Allyson Koerner, "Who Is Michael Phelps' Dad? The Olympic Swimmer Hasn't Always Had the Best Relationship with His Father," Bustle, August 4, 2016. www.bustle.com.
47. Phelps and Cazeneuve, *Beneath the Surface*, p. 165.
48. Phelps and Cazeneuve, *Beneath the Surface*, pp. 115–16.
49. Quoted in Tom Friend, "Next: LeBron James," *ESPN the Magazine*, December 10, 2002. www.espn.com.
50. Quoted in Matt McMillen, "LeBron James Pays Homage to the Mothers in His Life," WebMD. www.webmd.com.
51. Quoted in McMillen, "LeBron James Pays Homage to the Mothers in His Life."
52. Quoted in Friend, "Next."
53. Quoted in Mallory Chin, "LeBron James Reminisces on His Journey to Becoming the Face of the NBA," Hypebeast, September 11, 2017. https://hypebeast.com.

54. Quoted in Anna Bahr, "Selena Gomez Talks Parents' Divorce: 'I Blamed My Mom a Lot,'" *Huffington Post*, June 30, 2011. www.huffingtonpost.com.

55. Quoted in Bahr, "Selena Gomez Talks Parents' Divorce."

56. Quoted in "Selena Gomez Talks About Her Difficult Childhood," PerezHilton.com, June 20, 2011. http://perezhilton.com.

57. Quoted in Just Jared Jr., "Selena Gomez: 'My Mom Is My Happiness,'" April 22, 2009. www.justjaredjr.com.

58. Quoted in Chuck Barney, "Selena Gomez Could Be Next Disney 'It' Girl," *San Francisco East Bay Times*, February 7, 2008. www.eastbaytimes.com.

Chapter Five: What It Is like When My Family Grows

59. Sabrina Toucinho, "Dating and the Single Parent," *Divorce Magazine*, May 17, 2017. www.divorcemag.com.

60. Quoted in Johnson and Rosenfeld, *Divorced Kids*, p. 195.

61. Quoted in Hello Grief, "Teens' Talk About Parents Dating Again," Hello Grief, March 2014. www.hellogrief.org.

62. Ron L. Deal, "11 'Best Practices' for Dating as a Single Parent," Family Life, 2017. www.familylife.com.

63. Quoted in Edelman, *Motherless Daughters*, p. 126.

64. Quoted in Hello Grief, "Teens' Talk About Parents Dating Again."

65. Quoted in Johnson and Rosenfeld, *Divorced Kids*, p. 192.

66. Quoted in Robertson, *He Never Came Home*, p. 32.

67. Quoted in Johnson and Rosenfeld, *Divorced Kids*, p. 202.

68. Quoted in Johnson and Rosenfeld, *Divorced Kids*, pp. 202–03.

69. Quoted in Edelman, *Motherless Daughters*, p. 127.

70. Quoted in Heather Hetchler, "The Stepmom and Stepdaughter Jealousy Dance," Café Smom, July 29, 2012. http://wordpress.cafesmom.com.

71. Quoted in Robertson, *He Never Came Home*, p. 97.

72. Quoted in Robertson, *He Never Came Home*, p. 134.

73. Sharmayne, comment on Circle of Moms, "Half-Siblings," April 1, 2010. www.circleofmoms.com.

For Further Research

Books

Timothy Callahan and Claudia Isler, *A Teen's Guide to Custody*. New York: Rosen, 2016.

Roman Espejo, *Divorce and Children*. Farmington Hills, MI: Greenhaven, 2015.

Greenhaven, *Single-Parent Families*. Farmington Hills, MI: Greenhaven, 2016.

Paula Morrow, *My Parents Are Divorcing. Now What?* New York: Rosen, 2015.

H.W. Poole, *Single-Parent Families*. Broomall, PA: Mason Crest, 2016.

Samantha Waltz, ed., *Blended: Writers on the Stepfamily Experience*. Berkeley, CA: Seal, 2015.

Internet Sources

Alexandra D'Aluisio, "10 Celebrities Whose Dad Abandoned Them Before They Became Famous," Clevver, January 9, 2016. www.clevver.com/celebrities-abandoned-by-father-dad-who-left /nggallery/image/demi-lovato-230.

John Kelly, "Does Single Parenting Affect Children?," HowStuffWorks, 2017. https://lifestyle.howstuffworks.com/family/parenting /single-parents/single-parenting-affect-children.htm.

Kids' Health, "Single Parent Families," July 10, 2017. www.cyh .com/HealthTopics/HealthTopicDetailsKids.aspx?p=335&np =282&id=2862.

Organizations and Websites

All Parenting (www.allparenting.com). This website provides a wide array of articles aimed at helping parents and families. It has a variety of articles aimed at single-parent families, including personal stories, statistics, and helpful advice.

Institute for Family Studies (https://ifstudies.org). The Institute for Family Studies supports research and education that helps children and strengthens all types of families. The website has a variety of articles and reports about life in single-parent families.

Livestrong.com (www.livestrong.com). Livestrong.com helps people lead healthy lives. It has articles related to a variety of issues affecting single-parent families, including the psychological and economic effects on children of growing up in these families.

The Spruce (www.thespruce.com). The Spruce is a website that provides information related to family life. The Single Parent section offers a wide variety of articles and personal stories about child custody, visitation, child support, and census data, among other issues affecting single-parent families.

US Census Bureau (www.census.gov). The US Census Bureau gathers data about life in the United States. The website has a variety of statistics and infographics related to single-parent families.

Index